Aberdeen F(
Quiz Book

101 Questions That Will Test Y
Of Aberdeen Football Club

Published by Glowworm Press
7 Nuffield Way, Abingdon OX14 1RL
By Chris Carpenter

Aberdeen Football Club

This book contains one hundred and one informative and entertaining trivia questions with multiple choice answers. With 101 questions, some easy, some more demanding, this entertaining book will really test your knowledge of Aberdeen Football Club.

You will be quizzed on a wide range of topics associated with Aberdeen Football Club for you to test yourself, with questions on players, managers, transfer deals, trophies, records and more, guaranteeing you a truly educational experience. This **Aberdeen FC** Quiz Book will provide the ultimate in entertainment for fans of all ages and it is a must-have for all loyal Aberdeen supporters.

2020/21 Season Edition

FOREWORD

When I was asked to write a foreword to this book I was deeply honoured.

I have known Chris for many years and his knowledge of facts and figures is absolutely phenomenal.

His love for football and his talent for writing quiz books makes him the ideal man to pay homage to my great love Aberdeen Football Club.

I know that this book has taken him some time to create, as there have been a lot of facts and figures to check; but I believe it has been worth waiting for.

I do hope you enjoy the book.

Scott McDonald

Let's start with some relatively easy questions.

1. When was Aberdeen FC founded?
   A. 1902
   B. 1903
   C. 1904

2. What is the club's nickname?
   A. The Accies
   B. The Bairns
   C. The Dons

3. Who has made the most appearances for the club in total?
   A. Bobby Clark
   B. Alex McLeish
   C. Willie Miller

4. How many appearances did he make?
   A. 737
   B. 767
   C. 797

5. Who has made the most *League* appearances for the club?
   A. Russel Anderson
   B. Stewart McKimmie
   C. Willie Miller

6. Who holds the record for most appearances as a goalkeeper for the club?
   A. Bobby Clark
   B. Jim Leighton
   C. Fred Martin

7. Who is the club's record goal scorer?
   A. Matt Armstrong
   B. George Hamilton

C. Joe Harper

8. Who is the club's record *League* goal scorer?
   A. Matt Armstrong
   B. George Hamilton
   C. Joe Harper

9. Who holds the record for most goals scored in a season?
   A. Drew Jarvie
   B. Mark McGhee
   C. Benny Yorston

10. How many goals did he score?
    A. 40
    B. 43
    C. 46

OK, so here are the answers to the first ten questions. If you get seven or more right, you are doing very well so far, but beware the questions will get harder.

A1. Aberdeen Football Club as we know it today was born out of the merger of three city clubs; Aberdeen, Victoria United and Orion. A public meeting on 20th March 1903 was attended by more than 1,600 people, when the amalgamation issue was discussed and given the go-ahead. On 14th April 1903 the merger was made official and Aberdeen Football Club was born.

A2. Aberdeen are known as "The Dons", a name that has been in use since at least 1913. The origin of this nickname is unclear. One theory is that it derives from the word "don" meaning "teacher", given Aberdeen's history as a university town. It may also be a reference to the nearby River Don, or a contraction of "Aberdonians".

A3. The player who has made the most appearances for Aberdeen is Willie Miller. He was once described by Sir Alex Ferguson as "the best penalty box defender in the world."

A4. Willie Miller signed full-time for Aberdeen in 1971 at the age of 16. His total of 797 competitive appearances for the club is comfortably (by more than 100 matches) the all-time record.

A5. The legend who has made the most League appearances for Aberdeen is Willie Miller, with a grand total of 561 appearances.

A6. Between 1965 and 1980, Bobby Clark played a record 594 games between the sticks in total for the club.

A7. Joe Harper is the club's record goal scorer, scoring a total of 199 goals during his two spells with the club (1969-1972 and 1976-1980).

A8. Joe Harper also holds the record for most League goals scored - with a grand total of 125.

A9. Benny Yorston has the record for most goals scored in a season.

A10. Yorston scored a total of 46 goals in total during the 1929-1930 season, including 38 goals in the League. It is a record that is unlikely to ever be broken.

Now we move onto some questions about the ground.

11. Where does Aberdeen FC play their home games?
    A. Pettedrie Stadium
    B. Pittodrie Stadium
    C. Putterdrum Stadiim

12. What is the club's record attendance?
    A. 45,061
    B. 46,106
    C. 47,016

13. What is the name of the road the ground is on?
    A. Ardarroch Road
    B. Golf Road
    C. Pittodrie Street

14. What is the stadium's current capacity?
    A. 20,866
    B. 22,866
    C. 24,866

15. What is the size of the pitch??
    A. 100 x 64 metres
    B. 100 x 65 metres
    C. 100 x 66 metres

16. What is the newest stand at the ground?
    A. Main
    B. Richard Donald
    C. South

17. Which of these is the name of a hospitality suite at the ground?
    A. Teddy Bear Lounge
    B. Teddy Scott Lounge
    C. Teddy Thompson Lounge

18. In 1978 what did the club proclaim as a first for the ground?
    A. First electronic scoreboard in the UK
    B. First all covered, all seated stadium in the UK
    C. First set of rotating pitch side adverts in the UK

19. Which famous musicians have held concerts at the stadium?
    A. Elton John and Rod Stewart
    B. Madonna and Pink
    C. Prince and Usher

20. How many times has the stadium hosted Scotland international matches?
    A. 14
    B. 15
    C. 16

Here are the answers to the last set of questions.

A11. Pittodrie Stadium, commonly referred to as Pittodrie, was first used in 1899 and from 1903, has been the home of Aberdeen FC. Pittodrie is the fourth largest stadium in the SPFL and the largest stadium in Scotland outside the Central Belt. From 1899 to 1968 it was known as Pittodrie Park. There are plans to develop a new stadium close to the newly developed Aberdeen Western Peripheral Route.

A12. The club's record home attendance is 45,061 for a match against Hearts on 13th March 1954.

A13. The stadium is located on Pittodrie Street, very close to the City Centre.

A14. In addition to its main role of hosting home matches for Aberdeen FC, the Pittodrie Stadium has been the venue for a number of Scottish International matches and occasional games of rugby and currently has a capacity of 20,866.

A15. The pitch is 100 metres long and 66 metres wide which is 109 yards long by 72 yards wide.

A16. The Richard Donald Stand, also known as the Dick Donald or RDS stand, was the latest stand to be built at the ground, being completed in 1993. It holds some 6,000 spectators, all seated.

A17. The Teddy Scott Lounge is a hospitality suite available on a match by match basis. You will get a pre-match meal, half time refreshments, a post-match snack and padded seats in the Dick Donald stand. It's affordable and it's worth it to treat your lad to a memorable day, or if you want to get a group of guys, and girls for that matter together, to mark a special occasion. The suite is named after Teddy Scott who served Aberdeen in a number of "behind the scenes" capacities in his

49 years at the club. He was held in such high esteem he was even awarded the honour of a testimonial match in 1999.

A18. In 1978, Pittodrie became the first all seated, all covered stadium in the United Kingdom. It sounds grand, but the reality was that wooden bench seating was bolted to the terraces, and the southern corners of the ground remained open to the skies.

A19. On 19th June, 2004 Elton John played his only Scottish show at Pittodrie in front of a capacity crowd of 26,000 people, while Rod Stewart has rocked the stadium on several occasions.

A20. Since its construction, there have been fifteen Scotland international matches staged at Pittodrie. Normally the national team's home matches are played at Hampden Park in Glasgow, but during times of redevelopment of the national stadium, or to widen the audience for the national side, the Scottish Football Association has made use of other stadia in the country. Playing at Pittodrie, Scotland have won ten matches, drawn two and lost three. The most recent match was a 1–0 loss to The Netherlands on 9th November 2017.

OK, back to the questions.

21. What is the club's record win in all competitions?
    A. 11-0
    B. 12-0
    C. 13-0

22. What is the club's record League win?
    A. 8-0
    B. 9-0
    C. 10-0

23. What is the club's record defeat?
    A. 0-7
    B. 0-8
    C. 0-9

24. What is the highest transfer fee received by the club?
    A. £1,550,000
    B. £1,750,000
    C. £1,950,000

25. Who was the record transfer fee received for?
    A. Eoin Jess
    B. Fred Martin
    C. Niall McGinn

26. What is the highest transfer fee paid by the club?
    A. £1,000,000
    B. £1,250,000
    C. £1,500,000

27. Who was the record transfer fee paid for?
    A. Paul Bernard
    B. Norrie Davidson
    C. Andy Love

28. What is the record number of spectators to ever watch a game involving Aberdeen?
    A. 143,536
    B. 145,653
    C. 147,365

29. Who was the first Aberdeen player to be capped by Scotland?
    A. Willie Lennie
    B. Max Lowe
    C. Adam Rooney

30. Who was the oldest player to make his debut for Scotland?
    A. Donald Colman
    B. Neil Gibson
    C. Jimmy Millar

Here are the answers to the last set of questions.

A21. The club's record win is 13-0. It was a Scottish Cup 3rd Round match at home to Peterhead on 10th February 1923.

A22. The club's record league win is 10-0. It was a match played at Pittodrie Stadium against Raith Rovers in Scottish Division One on 13th October 1962.

A23. On 6th November 2010, Celtic beat Aberdeen 9-0 in a Scottish Premier League match, the biggest defeat ever suffered by the club.

A24. Aberdeen's record transfer fee received was £1,750,000 from Coventry City in February 1996.

A25. Aberdeen's record transfer fee received was for Eoin Jess. During his time at Aberdeen, Jess made 380 appearances for the club; and he has been described as "arguably the club's last great player".

A26. Aberdeen's record transfer fee paid is just £1,000,000; way back in September 1995.

A27. The record fee was paid to Oldham Athletic for midfielder Paul Bernard, who went on to play 100 times for the Dons.

A28. The 1937 Scottish Cup Final between Aberdeen and Celtic was watched by a European record domestic crowd of 147,365 at Hampden Park.

A29. Winger Willie Lennie became the first Aberdeen player to be capped by Scotland when he represented his country in an international match against Northern Ireland on 14th March1908.

A30. Donald Colman became the oldest Aberdeen player to make his debut for Scotland when he played against Wales on

6th March 1911 at the age of 32 years and 202 days. Colman was a tough tackling right back who went on to make a total of four appearances for Scotland.

I hope you're learning some new facts about the club, and here is the next set of questions.

31. How many times have Aberdeen won the Scottish League?
   A. 3
   B. 4
   C. 5

32. When did Aberdeen win the Scottish League for the first time?
   A. 1953-54
   B. 1954-55
   C. 1955-56

33. How many times have Aberdeen won the Scottish Cup?
   A. 3
   B. 5
   C. 7

34. When was the last time Aberdeen won the Scottish Cup?
   A. 1988
   B. 1989
   C. 1990

35. How many times have Aberdeen won the Scottish League Cup?
   A. 5
   B. 6
   C. 7

36. Who is the fastest ever goal scorer for the club?
   A. John Hewitt
   B. Adan Rooney
   C. Lee Wallace

37. Who has scored the most goals in European competitions?

A. John Hewitt
B. Drew Jarvis
C. Mark McGhee

38. Who won the most caps as an Aberdeen player?
    A. Matt Armstrong
    B. Fred Martin
    C. Alex McLeish

39. Who was the first Aberdeen player to play at a World Cup tournament?
    A. Fred Martin
    B. Adam Rooney
    C. Duncan Shearer

40. Who is the youngest player to make his debut for the club?
    A. Dean Campbell
    B. Bobby Clark
    C. Jack Grimmer

Here are the answers to the last block of questions.

A31. The club has won the Scottish League four times.

A32. The first time Aberdeen won the Scottish League was during the 1954/55 season.

A33. The Scottish Football Association Challenge Cup, commonly known as the Scottish Cup, has been won seven times by the club.

A34. 1990 was the last time the club won the Scottish Cup. It was the first cup final to have been decided by a penalty shootout. On 12th May 1990 Aberdeen drew 0-0 with Celtic over 90 minutes of normal play and 30 minutes of extra-time. The resulting penalty shoot-out was very dramatic with Aberdeen emerging victorious by winning the shootout 9-8.

A35. Aberdeen has won the Scottish League Cup six times, the first time in season 1955-56 and the last time in 2013-14.

A36. On 23rd January 1982, John Hewitt scored the only goal of the game in a third round Scottish Cup tie against Motherwell at Fir Park. His goal, timed at 9.6 seconds, was the fastest goal ever recorded in Scottish Cup history. Hewitt was later inducted into the Aberdeen Hall of Fame as one of the founding members.

A37. Mark McGee holds the record for most goals scored in European competition, with 14 goals in total.

A38. Alex McLeish is the most capped Aberdeen player. He won 77 caps for Scotland.

A39. Goalkeeper Fred Martin was the first Aberdeen player to represent Scotland at a World Cup tournament when he played for Scotland against Austria in Zurich, Switzerland on

16th June 1954 during their first ever FIFA World Cup finals appearance.

A40. Dean Campbell made his professional debut for Aberdeen in a league match against Celtic on 12th May 2017, aged just 16 years and 51 days. Earlier the same day he sat an English exam at his school.

Here are some questions about the club's achievements in European football.

41. How many European trophies has the club won?
    A. 1
    B. 2
    C. 3

42. In which year did Aberdeen win the European Cup Winners Cup?
    A. 1982
    B. 1983
    C. 1984

43. Who did they beat in the final?
    A. Atletico Madrid
    B. Inter Milan
    C. Real Madrid

44. What was the score?
    A. 1-0
    B. 2-1
    C. 3-2

45. Who scored the winning goal?
    A. Eric Black
    B. John Hewitt
    C. Neil Simpson

46. In which stadium did this game take place?
    A. Camp Nou Stadium
    B. Nya Ullevi Stadium
    C. San Siro Stadium

47. Who was the captain who led the team to victory?
    A. Joe Harper
    B. Mark McGhee
    C. Willie Miller

48. What was the team known as?
      A. The Gothenburg Giants
      B. The Gothenburg Glory Boys
      C. The Gothenburg Greats

49. When did the club win the UEFA Super Cup?
      A. 1981
      B. 1982
      C. 1983

50. Who did they beat in the two legged final?
      A. Hamburger SV
      B. Lazio
      C. PSG

Here are the answers to the last set of questions.

A41. Aberdeen has won a total of 2 European trophies: The UEFA Cup Winner's Cup and the UEFA Super Cup. They are actually the only Scottish team to have won two European trophies.

A42. Aberdeen FC won their first European trophy – the European Cup Winner's Cup, in 1983, on 11th May 1983 to be precise.

A43. Aberdeen beat Spanish giants Real Madrid in the final.

A44. Aberdeen won the match 2-1 after extra time.

A45. At the end of normal time, the score was 1-1. The match went into extra time, with the winning goal being scored for Aberdeen by John Hewitt in the 112th minute.

A46. The final was held at Nya Ullevi Stadium in Gothenburg, Sweden.

A47. The captain of the winning team was Willie Miller, the player who also made a club record of 560 league appearances for Aberdeen.

A48. The team became known as the Gothenburg Greats.

A49. Aberdeen FC won the UEFA Super Cup trophy in 1983.

A50. The 1983 UEFA Super Cup was a two legged match contested between the European Cup Champions Hamburger SV and the European Cup Winners Cup Champions Aberdeen. The first leg was a 0-0 draw played on 22nd November 1983 in Hamburg, and the return leg was played on 20th December 1983 at Pittodrie, where Aberdeen won 2-0 with goals coming from Mark McGhee and Neil Simpson. Aberdeen are the only Scottish team to ever win the UEFA Super Cup.

I hope you're learning some new facts about the club, and here is the next set of questions.

51. Who is the current official kit supplier?
    A. Adidas
    B. Le Coq Sportif
    C. Nike

52. Who was the first official kit supplier in 1975?
    A. Bukta
    B. Puma
    C. Umbro

53. Who is the current club sponsor?
    A. Apex Tubulars
    B. Saltire Energy
    C. Team Recruitment

54. Who was the first shirt sponsor?
    A. JVC
    B. Samsung
    C. Sony

55. Who is the current Chairman?
    A. Dave Cormack
    B. Stewart Milne
    C. Robert Wicks

56. Who is the current Club Ambassador?
    A. Craig Brown
    B. Darren Eales
    C. Duncan Fraser

57. Who is the club mascot?
    A. Angus the Bull
    B. Donald the Golfer
    C. Roger the Roughneck

58. What is the name of the official match day programme?
   A. Aberdeen View
   B. Official Match Day Magazine
   C. RedMatchDay

59. What is the official website address?
   A. aberdeenfc.co.uk
   B. afc.co.uk
   C. aberdeen.com

60. What is the club's official twitter account?
   A. @AberdeenFC
   B. @FCAberdeen
   C. @AberdeenOfficial

Here are the answers to the last block of questions.

A51. Global sports giant Adidas is the official kit supplier and has been since 2011.

A52. The first official team kit supplier was Bukta who first supplied the team during the 1975/76 season.

A53. Saltire Energy are the current shirt sponsors. They are an oilfield equipment rental company.

A54. JVC was Aberdeen's first ever shirt sponsor, back in 1987.

A55. Dave Cormack is the current chairman of Aberdeen Football Club, a position he has held since December 2019.

A56. Craig Brown is employed by the club as its Club Ambassador.

A57. The club mascot is Angus the Bull. He enjoys goofing around before the games, and he is known to the staff as Bully. More recently Donny the sheep has been introduced as well. Give yourself a bonus point if you knew that.

A58. RedMatchDay is the name of the official Aberdeen FC match day programme.

A59. afc.co.uk is the official website address.

A60. @AberdeenFC is the official twitter account of the club. It tweets multiple times per day and it now has over 100,000 followers.

Here is the next set of questions.

61. Who was the first manager of the club?
    A. Dave Halliday
    B. Jimmy Philip
    C. Paddy Travers

62. How many foreign managers (non UK) have the club had in total?
    A. 1
    B. 2
    C. 3

63. How many Englishmen have managed Aberdeen?
    A. 0
    B. 1
    C. 2

64. Who started the 2020-21 season as manager?
    A. Stuart Duff
    B. Mark McGee
    C. Derek McInnes

65. Who started the 2020-21 season as assistant manager?
    A. Tony Docherty
    B. Graham Kirk
    C. Paul Sheerin

66. In August 2010 who scored a hat-trick of penalties?
    A. Sone Aluko
    B. Paul Hartley
    C. Chris Maguire

67. How many seasons has the club spent outside the top division?
    A. 0
    B. 1
    C. 2

68. What was the nickname of George Campbell?
     A. The Cannon Ball
     B. Little Mozart
     C. White Pele

69. Which Aberdeen player carries the title of the youngest
    goal scorer in the Scottish Premier League?
     A. Fraser Fyvie
     B. Stephen Glass
     C. Bob Wishart

70. Who were the opponents in the first game that
    Aberdeen ever played?
     A. Alloa
     B. Dunfermline
     C. Stenhousemuir

Here are the answers to the last block of questions.

A61. Jimmy Philip was the very first manager of the club. He was in charge of the club from its foundation in 1903 until his retirement in 1924.

A62. Aberdeen's first and only foreign manager Ebbe Skovdahl was appointed in July 1999. The Dane worked with a very restricted budget and managed the club for three and a half seasons before resigning in November 2002.

A63. Keith Burkinshaw is the only Englishman to have ever manged Aberdeen. He was appointed as a caretaker-manager in 1997 following the sacking of Roy Aitken and his reign lasted just two matches before Alex Miller was appointed to the role.

A64. Derek McInnes started the 2020-21 season as manager, a role he has held since March 2013. In his first season as manager, Aberdeen won the 2014 Scottish League Cup, the club's first trophy in 19 years.

A65. Tony Docherty started the 2020-21 campaign as assistant manager.

A66. Paul Hartley made history by becoming the first player to score a hat trick of penalties in the Scottish Premier League in the 4-0 victory over Hamilton on 14th August 2010.

A67. The club has spent its entire existence in the top division.

A68. George Campbell spent seven seasons at Aberdeen from 1972 to 1978 as a left-sided midfielder and was nicknamed the 'White Pele' and 'The Pele of the North' because of his unique skill on the ball.

A69. Fraser Fyvie scored his first senior goal for Aberdeen aged just 16 years and 306 days on 27th January 2010, against

Hearts at Tynecastle to become the youngest goal scorer in the Scottish Premier League.

A70. On 15th August 1903, approximately 8,000 spectators watched Aberdeen FC play its first game at Pittodrie, a 1-1 draw in the Northern League against Stenhousemuir.

Here is the next batch of ten carefully chosen questions.

71. What is the traditional colour of the home shirt?
    A. All red
    B. Red and white quarters
    C. Red and white stripes

72. What is the traditional colour of the away shirt?
    A. Gold
    B. White
    C. Yellow

73. What world first can Pittodrie lay claim to?
    A. First dug-out
    B. First floodlights
    C. First netting of goals

74. Who was the chairman of Aberdeen throughout the 1980s?
    A. Richard Donald
    B. Tom Farmer
    C. Alex Ferguson

75. With whom does Aberdeen contest the so called North Derby with?
    A. Arbroath
    B. Brechin City
    C. Inverness

76. In which season did Aberdeen first participate in a European competition?
    A. 1966-67
    B. 1967-68
    C. 1968-69

77. Who was Aberdeen's opponent in their first competitive European match?
    A. Honved

B. KR Reykjavik

C. Real Zaragoza

78. Who did Aberdeen eliminate during the quarter-finals of the European Cup Winners Cup in 1983?
    A. Austria Vienna
    B. Barcelona
    C. Bayern Munich

79. What is Marc De Clerck most famous for?
    A. Breaking his leg on his debut
    B. Getting sent off on his debut
    C. Scoring on his debut

80. When did Aberdeen open the Hall of Fame?
    A. 2002
    B. 2004
    C. 2006

Here is the latest set of answers.

A71. The traditional colour of the home shirt is red. In 1939 the club changed the previously worn first choice of black and gold stripes to red, to reflect the red and silver colours of the official City of Aberdeen arms.

A72. The most frequently used colour of the away shirt is white, often paired with black shorts.

A73. Pittodrie was the first stadium to feature a dug-out, an invention of Donald Colman. Years ahead of his time, Colman was an innovative coach who was convinced of the importance of watching his players' feet, and to help with this, he devised the dugout, a sheltered area, set below pitch level. The idea spread throughout the world, but incredibly it was Pittodrie that was the first to have a dug-out.

A74. Richard Donald was the chairman of the club throughout the 1980s – the most successful period in the club's history.

A75. The match between Aberdeen and Inverness Caledonian Thistle is considered to be the "North Derby" and it has arisen since Inverness were first promoted to the SPL in 2004.

A76. Aberdeen's first participation in European competition was in the 1967-68 season, when they competed in the UEFA Cup Winners' Cup.

A77. Aberdeen played their first official match in competitive European football on 6th September 1967 in a UEFA Cup Winners' Cup first-round game against KR Reykjavik of Iceland. The match ended in a 10-0 victory for Aberdeen. The return leg saw Aberdeen win 4-1, making the score 14-1 on aggregate.

A78. In the quarter-finals Aberdeen were drawn against Bayern Munich. The first leg, in Germany, was a 0-0 draw. In the return leg in Scotland on the 16th March 1983 Aberdeen went through with a 3-2 victory. The pulsating game has become known as "Pittodrie's greatest night." It is worth tracking it down on YouTube to see why.

A79. On 30th August 1980 The Dons beat Berwick in the League Cup 4-1, but the game was remembered for an astonishing goal from Aberdeen's debutant goalkeeper Marc De Clerck when one of his clearances bounced once and over Berwick goalkeeper Davidson and into the goal.

A80. The Aberdeen Hall of Fame was established in 2004 with the purpose to formally acknowledge the players and staff that have reached the pinnacle of their profession and made a significant contribution to the club.

Here are the next set of questions, and let's hope you get most of them right.

81. Where is the new stadium and training facility being developed?
    A. Kingsford
    B. King's Links
    C. Kingswells

82. Who received the Scottish PFA Players' Player of the year award in 1982?
    A. Davie Robb
    B. George Hamilton
    C. Mark McGhee

83. What is the name of the song that was performed by the Aberdeen squad in 1983?
    A. Aberdeen High
    B. European Song
    C. Northern Lights

84. What is the nickname of Derek McKay?
    A. Cup-tie McKay
    B. Pit-bull McKay
    C. Speed-king McKay

85. How many players were involved in each of Aberdeen's three Scottish Cup Finals in a row in the 1980s?
    A. 5
    B. 7
    C. 9

86. What position did the club finish at the end of the 2019-20 season?
    A. 3rd
    B. 4th
    C. 5th

87. Who was voted the player of the year for the 2019-20 season?
    A. Dean Campbell
    B. Andrew Considine
    C. Joe Lewis

88. Who was the leading scorer for the 2019-20 season?
    A. Sam Cosgrove
    B. Niall McGinn
    C. Connor McLellan

89. What shirt number does Lewis Ferguson wear?
    A. 15
    B. 17
    C. 19

90. Which of these is a well-known pub near the ground?
    A. The Bobbin
    B. The Dobbin
    C. The Robbin

Here are the answers to the last block of questions.

A81. The board have stated that Pittodrie is a land locked site and any redevelopment would cost more than a new purpose built stadium with training facilities. The site chosen for the new stadium is at Kingsford, some six miles to the West of the city centre. Following a judicial review, the new stadium plan has been approved and construction on the road access and also the training complex is ongoing. Of course, there is a long way to go yet, and there remains the question of how the club will finance the anticipated £50 million cost of the new stadium.

A82. Mark McGhee won the Scottish PFA Players' Player of the Year award in 1982.

A83 "European Song" is a football song released in 1983 to mark Aberdeen's participation in the 1983 European Cup Winners' Cup Final. It was performed by the Aberdeen squad and written by Harry Barry. It would be fair to say it was not the best football song ever recorded!

A84. Derek McKay earned the nickname "Cup-tie McKay", because of his goals which were scored during the club's glory run to lift the Scottish Cup in 1970. McKay scored the winning goals in the quarter-final and semi-final matches, before scoring twice in the 3-1 Final win over favourites Celtic. He left Aberdeen just three matches later after a row over bonuses for the Cup Final.

A85. When Aberdeen won three Scottish Cups in a row (4-1 over Rangers in 1982, 1-0 over Rangers in 1983 and 2-1 over Celtic in 1984) an incredible total of nine players were involved in all three Finals. They were:- Jim Leighton, Doug Rougvie, Neil Simpson, Willie Miller, Alex McLeish, Gordon Strachan, Neale Cooper, Mark McGhee and Eric Black. It demonstrates the benefits of a settled side.

A86. Aberdeen finished the 2019-20 season in fourth place, some way behind champions Celtic.

A87. After a fantastic season, Andrew Considine was voted the player of the year for the 2019-20 season.

A88. During the 2019-20 season Sam Cosgrove was the leading goalscorer with 23 goals in total, including 11 in the League.

A89. Midfielder Lewis Ferguson wears shirt number 19.

A90. The Bobbin is one of the close boozers to the ground, being just a few minutes' walk away. Be prepared to queue for a pint though.

Here is the final set of questions. Enjoy!

91 Who started the 2020-21 season as club captain?
    A. Joe Lewis
    B. Scott McKenna
    C. Graeme Shinnie

92. What is the number of his shirt?
    A. 1
    B. 13
    C. 20

93. What nationality is goalkeeper Joe Lewis?
    A. English
    B. Irish
    C. Welsh

94. What shirt number does Shay Logan wear?
    A. 2
    B. 3
    C. 4

95. How many of the 1983 Cup Winners Cup Final side were named in the "Greatest Ever XI" in 2015?
    A. 4
    B. 5
    C. 6

96. Which team did Aberdeen beat in the 1947 Scottish Cup Final?
    A. Hearts
    B. Hibernian
    C. Motherwell

97. What is the official club crest?
    A. Capital letter A with a ball forming a crossbar
    B. Four leaf clover
    C. Lion rampant

98. Which of these is a song associated with the club?
    A. I dream of sheep
    B. The sheep are on fire
    C. The year of the sheep

99. How many Aberdeen players have gone on to become Scotland national football team manager (excluding caretaker roles)?
    A. 2
    B. 3
    C. 4

100. Who was the manager of the 1983 Cup Winners Cup winning team?
    A. Alex Ferguson
    B. Ally MacLeod
    C. Billy McNeill

101. How many of the eleven players in the 1983 Cup Winners Cup Final team were Scottish?
    A. 9
    B. 10
    C. 11

Here are the answers to the final block of questions.

A91. Joe Lewis started the 2020-21 season as club captain.

A92. Goalkeeper Lewis wears the number 1 shirt.

A93. Joe Lewis is English, having been born in Bury St Edmunds in Suffolk.

A94. Shaleum "Shay" Logan wears shirt number 2.

A95. In November 2015, the club's Greatest Ever Xi was named after a poll amongst Red Army supporters. The Greatest XI named were Jim Leighton, Willie Miller, Alex McLeish, Stuart Kennedy, Neil Simpson, Russell Anderson, Gordon Strachan, Jim Bett, Eoin Jess, Joe Harper, Duncan Shearer. So, five of these eleven started the 1983 Cup Winners Cup Final.

A96. Aberdeen defeated Hibernian 2-1 in the 1947 Scottish Cup Final to gain the club's first major trophy.

A97. Starting from 1972, the official crest design represented a capital letter *A* as the side view of a football goal, with a ball forming the crossbar of the letter signifying the scoring of a goal. The logo was completed by the letters *FC* in smaller type at a level with the ball element. Two stars signifying the winning of two European trophies were introduced over the badge from the 2005-06 season onwards.

A98. "The sheep are on fire" is a song associated with the club.

A99. Two Aberdeen players have gone on to manage the national team. They are Gordon Strachan and Alex McLeish. Billy Stark managed Scotland in a caretaker role for one match in 2012.

A100. The manager that season was Alex Ferguson. During his years of management at the club between 1978 and 1986, Aberdeen also won the European Super Cup, three League Championships, four Scottish Cups, a League Cup and a Drybrough Cup; all in the space of seven years. Sir Alex Ferguson is naturally the most successful manager in the club's history.

A101 All of the eleven players who played in the 1983 European Cup Winners Cup Final were Scottish. As were all five of the substitutes. How times have changed. Another surprising statistic, and a good one to finish this book on, is the Gothenburg eleven only ever started two matches – and won two cups!

That's it. That's a great question to finish on. I hope you enjoyed this book, and I hope you got most of the answers right. I also hope you learnt one or two new things about the club.

If you saw anything wrong, or have a general comment, please visit the glowwormpress.com website.

Thanks for reading, and if you did enjoy the book, would you be so kind as leave a positive review on Amazon.

Printed in Great Britain
by Amazon